#love

a quote book

by gloria marie pelcher

Copyright © 2014 Gloria Marie Pelcher

All rights reserved. No portion of this book may be used or reproduced in any manner whatsoever without written permission of the author or Creative Bluebird except in the case of brief quotations embodied in critical articles and reviews.

The quotes in this book have been collected from multiple sources, and are assumed to be accurate as quoted in their original published forms. Although every effort has been made to verify the quotes and sources, the Publisher cannot guarantee their perfect accuracy. No endorsement of this book has been made by any individual mentioned in this quote book.

#love: a quote book

ISBN-13: 978-0692347720 (Creative Bluebird)

ISBN-10: 0692347720

#quotebooks™ is a trademark of

Creative Bluebird
www.creativebluebird.com

For book inquiries please visit
creativebluebird.com/contact

for

___

from

___

date

___

love

Know that you are loved, and will always be loved…

I carry your heart (I carry it in my heart).

E.E. Cummings

As he read, I fell in love the way you fall asleep: slowly, and then all at once.

John Green

I love you without knowing how, or when, or from where. I love you simply, without problems or pride: I love you in this way because I do not know any other way of loving but this, in which there is no I or you, so intimate that your hand upon my chest is my hand, so intimate that when I fall asleep your eyes close.

Pablo Neruda

Being deeply loved by someone gives you strength, while loving someone deeply gives you courage.

Lao Tzu

Love is that condition in which the happiness of another person is essential to your own.

Robert A. Heinlein

Love is like the wind, you can't see it but you can feel it.

Nicholas Sparks

We're all a little weird. And life is a little weird. And when we find someone whose weirdness is compatible with ours, we join up with them and fall into mutually satisfying weirdness—and call it love—true love.

Robert Fulghum

One is loved because one is loved. No reason is needed for loving.

         Paulo Coelho

If I had a flower for every time I thought of you...I could walk through my garden forever.

Alfred Tennyson

Last week the candle factory burned down. Everyone just stood around and sang, "Happy Birthday".

Steven Wright

Where there is love there is life.

Mahatma Gandhi

You know you're in love when you can't fall asleep because reality is finally better than your dreams.

        Dr. Seuss

Some day you will be old enough to start reading fairy tales again.

C.S. Lewis

Nobody has ever measured, not even poets, how much the heart can hold.

Zelda Fitzgerald

Two people in love, alone, isolated from the world, that's beautiful.
Milan Kundera

Every heart sings a song, incomplete, until another heart whispers back.

Plato

There is always some madness in love. But there is also always some reason in madness.

Friedrich Nietzsche

For the two of us, home isn't a place. It is a person. And we are finally home.

Stephanie Perkins

Love doesn't just sit there, like a stone, it has to be made, like bread; remade all the time, made new.

Ursula K. Le Guin

We loved with a love that was more than love.

Edgar Allan Poe

And now these three remain: faith, hope and love. But the greatest of these is love.

The Bible

It was love at first sight, at last sight, at ever and ever sight.

Vladimir Nabokov

I love you also means I love you more than anyone loves you, or has loved you, or will love you, and also, I love you in a way that no one loves you, or has loved you, or will love you, and also, I love you in a way that I love no one else, and never have loved anyone else, and never will love anyone else.

Jonathan Safran Foer

One love, one heart, one destiny.

Bob Marley

Of all forms of caution, caution in love is perhaps the most fatal to true happiness.
Bertrand Russell

If you remember me, then I don't care if everyone else forgets.
Haruki Murakami

Look after my heart - I've left it with you.

Stephenie Meyer

We'll never be as young as we are tonight.

Chuck Palahniuk

You don't love someone because they're perfect, you love them in spite of the fact that they're not.

Jodi Picoult

How do you spell 'love'? - Piglet
You don't spell it...you feel it. - Pooh
A.A. Milne

When I saw you I fell in love, and you smiled because you knew.

Arrigo Boito

Who, being loved, is poor?

Oscar Wilde

One word
Frees us of all the weight and pain
of life:
That word is love.

Sophocles

The heart has its reasons
which reason knows not.
        Blaise Pascal

As if you were on fire from within. The moon lives in the lining of your skin.
       Pablo Neruda

To lose balance sometimes for love is part of living a balanced life.

Elizabeth Gilbert

Romance is the glamour which turns the dust of everyday life into a golden haze.

Elinor Glyn

Come sleep with me: We won't make Love, Love will make us.

Julio Cortázar

Be with me always - take any form -
drive me mad! Only do not leave me in
this abyss, where I cannot find you!
Emily Brontë

If we have no peace, it is because we have forgotten that we belong to each other.

Mother Teresa

Even
After
All this time
The Sun never says to the Earth,
"You owe me."
Look
What happens
With a love like that,
It lights the whole sky.

حاف ظ

Each of us is born with a box of matches inside us but we can't strike them all by ourselves.

Laura Esquivel

In your light I learn how to love. In your beauty, how to make poems. You dance inside my chest where no-one sees you, but sometimes I do, and that sight becomes this art.
Rumi

Every year on your birthday,
you get a chance to start new.

Sammy Hagar

Love has nothing to do with what you are expecting to get - only with what you are expecting to give - which is everything.

Katharine Hepburn

You don't love someone because of their looks or their clothes or their car. You love them because they sing a song only your heart can understand.

L.J. Smith

Love is a decision, it is a judgment, it is a promise. If love were only a feeling, there would be no basis for the promise to love each other forever. A feeling comes and it may go. How can I judge that it will stay forever, when my act does not involve judgment and decision.

Erich Fromm

If a thing loves, it is infinite.
William Blake

True love is not so much a matter of romance as it is a matter of anxious concern for the well-being of one's companion.

Gordon B. Hinckley

I am weird, you are weird. Everyone in this world is weird. One day two people come together in mutual weirdness and fall in love.

Dr. Seuss

my favorite love quote

_____
_____
_____
_____
_____
_____
_____
_____
_____
_____

ABOUT this book

THIS BOOK that you are holding in your hands was made with love by GLORIA MARIE PELCHER. This book is part of the *#quotebooks*™ collection of books. This book is perfectly okay with being loved, bought, read, reread, shared, gifted, tweeted, instagrammed, liked, reviewed, borrowed, and of course quoted.

gloriamarie.com/quotebooks

FB / IG / Twitter: @gloriamarie

www.ingramcontent.com/pod-product-compliance
Lightning Source LLC
Chambersburg PA
CBHW070459050426
42449CB00012B/3047